SUPERMAN
Doesn't Live Here Anymore
II

Run to Jesus

by Scott McPhillips

Mac on the Attack for Jesus
Honey Creek, IA

Mac on the Attack for Jesus
28535 Coldwater Avenue • Honey Creek, IA 51542

Although the author and publisher have made every effort to ensure the accuracy and completeness of information contained in this book, we assume no responsibility for errors, inaccuracies, omissions, or any inconsistency herein. Any slights of people, places, or organizations are unintentional.

First Printing 2007

ISBN-13: 978-0-9662205-9-9
ISBN-10: 0-9662205-9-5
LCCN: 2006907673

ATTENTION SPORTS ORGANIZATIONS, CORPORATIONS, UNIVERSITIES, COLLEGES, AND PROFESSIONAL ORGANIZATIONS: Quantity discounts are available on bulk purchases of this book for educational purposes. Special books or book excerpts can also be created to fit specific needs. For information, please contact:

Mac on the Attack for Jesus
28535 Coldwater Avenue • Honey Creek, IA 51542
Phone (712) 545-4477

Web site: hey-scott.com

CONTENTS

Where To Now?

Where to now, Lord Jesus?
You've got me on your way.
I'm just a seeking Christian
Searching your will today.

For all I lost, Lord Jesus,
I call it gain, not loss.
When I have failed you, Jesus,
Help me run to the Cross.

—*David Hufford*

What Happens When Superman Meets Jesus?

For some of us finding Christ may come after we have looked in all the wrong places: glory, athletic achievement, booze, drugs, sex, and gambling. Or we miss salvation because we are going too fast: being impatient, arguing, chasing around, looking for what we think is love, even trying to avoid God by living too fast. Or we may not know how to search for God:

"You will seek me and find me when you search for me with all your heart." Jeremiah 29:13

When we don't stop our running around, we may stop looking for God, and our pride may keep us from stopping to look for God. Pride, darkness, and a lead foot on the gas pedal may stop us more abruptly than the good reasons of our friends or our belief in our own thinking.

Our struggle begins after we have stopped. All of the above are true for Scott McPhillips.

I have known Scott for over twelve years. He came into my life about three years after his second and worst of two fateful wrecks and its terrible consequences, which he writes about in his first book, Superman Doesn't Live Here Anymore. I was, I admit, a bit quizzical when he asked me to write a chapter for that book; but I did have something to say, because I had known Scott for over two years; and we had had many discussions by that time, about life and the hard life, about love and lust, success and failure, drinking and drugging, and life disaster and recovery. And we talked about God.

At that time Scott was a student at Iowa Western Community College, where I was teaching, but our discussions almost never took the form or topic which would be called "academic." Any subject was open season, and our discussions spilled over from my office to outside of school. This book is a consequence of a conversation that has been going on for over twelve years. It is a discussion about God—not just theological Father-Son-Holy Spirit or moot points of the *Bible*, but a more pragmatic walking and talking with Jesus or like Paul. Since his hospital bed conversion, Scott has been walking the streets of Council Bluffs, Iowa and Omaha, Nebraska—and other places as far away from his home as Florida and the Bahamas, California, Mexico, and all over the Midwest—talking about Jesus, selling his first book, and doing his mission his way.

Scott and I now have a long conversational history (and I have met and talked with many of his family), and I have read his first book several times. I would not go so far as to say I know *what* Scott is thinking, but I know *how* he is thinking— which way the wind is blowing. So it is not puzzling to me that Scott would ask me to help him write his next book—this book.

My own spiritual walk has been of a more conventional kind: I have been actively involved in my own church for the past eighteen years, where I have been an adult Sunday School teacher and a choir member, among other tasks. But I would call myself a Child of God, a Christian, and a Lutheran. I have also been a teaching missionary in two other countries. But this is not my story.

Scott is also a child of God—there is no question about that. And Scott got his faith the hard way. But where I have been a missionary, Scott is a man with a mission. Scott has walked the streets where we live. Scott works with the spiritual urgency of one after a life disaster. I too have faced a life disaster, and I understand something of what Scott went through, but again this is not my story. Scott is unconventional, there is also no question about that. He is more visionary than most. And he speaks with the urgency of one who has met Jesus.

Why would somebody like that—and one who has already published a book—need me to help him write one?

I call Scott my "Man of Steel." That is a fitting metaphor for faith. It is, of course, the description of a Superman. In a harsher and more humble way it is Scott: a man fitted with steel plates, rods, bolts, and screws—literally a man of steel—and one who has had a hard journey back from physical disability. I am writing this book because Scott needs me to. He really can't write it himself—although some passages are painfully done by his own hand—excruciatingly slowly. Some parts were dictated to his mother. Some parts were dictated to me. I am simply the tool. Scott is the author. This is the story of what happens when Superman meets Jesus.

The journey really can continue.

—David Hufford, Believer, Writer, and Friend

Finding out That God Has a Plan for You (Even When You've Been Dead Wrong)

Lots of people never arrive where I am in life after they have been dead wrong. I was dead wrong, but I didn't die. After my second, and most tragic, wreck I had to experience life as a child would, learning to walk and talk and eat. But this is not that story.

This is the story of finding Jesus and making moral, spiritual, and religious progress. I had to begin there like a child, too. Well, isn't that the way we're supposed to begin? *"Truly I say to you, whoever does not receive the kingdom of God like a little child shall not enter it at all."* **Mark 10:15**

I used to follow sports first, women second, alcohol and drugs third; but if you worked it right, you could intertwine all of them together. That's how my life went until God got my attention. After my wreck and recovery, which I describe in detail in my first book, *Superman Doesn't Live Here Anymore*, I had a lot of spiritual growing to do. That's what this book is about. Here I speak often about how I mess up. But no matter in what way I mess up, the solution is to run to Jesus.

On my way to Jesus I often find that I must help others find Jesus too. To keep from messing up, I have to confront my demons. Whenever I seem to be getting back on track, Satan is right there. When I run to Jesus, there are others on the way. For me to get to the cross I must serve Christ by serving others. This book is about how I have learned to do that.

I know that everything I say is not politically correct, but I have worked very hard and am proud of what I have accomplished in this book. My overall goal is to lead as many people as I can to Jesus through showing them my mistakes, how an unrighteous man can find hope in Jesus.

First, I had to be changed. For me to change, I had to listen to God. To hear God, I had to learn to listen to God. Later I write about "Middle-of-the-Night Talks." That means what it says: it had to come down to a simple meeting in the silence of the night: God and me. That was necessary before I came to meet Jesus. But as you will see, first I will talk about the stumbling path I had to take to get there. Toward the end of the book I write about the road I am on today, and I invite you to follow me there.

It was a Thursday morning in May when Tom McMahon, a staff writer for the *Daily Nonpareil*, called me and asked me if he could do a follow-up story on my life from 1995. I said, "Sure."

And he said, "How about in an hour?"

I said, "let's do it, baby." The rest of the story written in the paper is found as an appendix in this book.

How I found out, after the article was published, was that my mother and I went to a restaurant in Crescent, Iowa, to have lunch, and the woman sitting next to me told me it was a good article. So my mother went to the corner store and got six copies for me. After reading the article, I was pleased with the job he did writing it. I was happy they included my talking with Jesus, and my mother's experience. I have to get on the ball now and keep working on this book for all the people who keep asking when this book will be published.

You do not say, "I want to write a book," and it magically happens. Like anything else, if you want it to be good, it takes a lot of hard, hard work. I've really enjoyed writing this book because of the person with whom I've been writing it: Mr. David Hufford. We've both been through a lot.

I need to give credit to the many people who have helped me along the way, above all, my mother who saw me through the darkest part of my life. Also I want to thank all the people who helped me write and produce my first book. If that book hadn't been written, this book couldn't be written. I thank all the people who have been with me through this book, especially David Hufford, who is helping me write it; my mother, again, who has helped check facts and dates and write passages legibly so that they may be transcribed; my pastor, Frank Farwell; my high school coach, Mr. Gaylord Schelling, who has helped me before and since my tragic accident, and who has written a testimonial printed in the appendix; and Tom McMahon, Staff Writer for the Council Bluffs' *Daily Nonpareil*, who has written two articles reproduced in the appendix.

I want to thank all the people who have taken dictation for me while I was writing this book. So many people have helped me, and I want to give a special thank-you to everyone. God will always be most important to me, but I know he places certain people in our lives to help us.

So, K.I.S.S. (keep it simple, stupid). Hopefully we will make the right choice and realize JESUS. gave his life for our sins. Accept Him and we will all party in heaven.

There will be people who oppose me and my thoughts, but that's OK. We are all created uniquely in God's image. I hope you all make it to heaven with me, and we will party—like never before—for eternity.

Jesus is worth it. Get to know Him.

I must also say something about the *Bible* I am using, the *New American Standard Annotated Bible* (NAS). All or nearly all quoted scripture is taken from the NAS unless otherwise noted. I use the NAS because I use many materials of Charles Stanley, and he says it is the most accurate and politically correct. I have a lot of Charles Stanley tapes. I listened to him a lot when I was a new believer. And my true thoughts and feelings are as follows: For new believers the New International Version (NIV) will give you an easier understanding of God than the

11

King James Bible. It is a good *Bible*. I used to be Lutheran, but I fell away from the Lutheran Church because the church I used to go to was the old Missouri Synod Lutheran. I am not a staunch person at all. I am a wild child for Jesus Christ.

I have read the NAS numerous times. I pick out something new I missed before every time. I'm still not as smart as I think I am.

Whatever *Bible* you choose to read is a good *Bible* as long as you read it; and the *Bible* you are reading praises the Triune God, and says Jesus Christ is the Son of God who died for all our sins, and the Holy Spirit, the still small voice in your head that tells you what way you should go. The Holy Spirit is God.

Whatever you are passionate about, do to the best of your ability. Praise God, and he will help you to succeed in whatever you do.

"Beloved, I pray that in all respects you may prosper and be in good health, just as your soul prospers." **3 John 2**

It is his will for you. He only wants the best for you.

This book is about how he proved that to me.

PROLOGUE

Getting Tired of the Consequences

I was very happy with the final printing of my first book. I have had many compliments from people who have read it. Who wouldn't like it? My overall objective in the first book was to introduce people to how I found God. All it shows is that we all need help. Not everyone has to learn the hard way like I did: I had to wake up and smell the coffee. I had to stop letting alcohol and drugs rule my life. You have to remember: you are the one in control, and you do not have to let alcohol and drugs run over you. Get help before what happened to me happens to you.

Many people, myself included, have had to hit rock bottom before they said, "I have to change." Now, there are real possibilities and plans in my life with the help of Jesus Christ, my Lord and Savior. You have your own choice. You can either learn from this, or say it is hogwash. The choice is yours. If you're happy, OK. If not, change.

It is a lot easier to see someone burn their hand on a hot stove than do it yourself. I love everyone, and hope people learn from my mistakes. Ultimately, the final result of sin is death. You play, you pay. Do your best, pray that it is blessed, and let God take care of the rest. How much does Jesus love you? He died for your sins.

It is easy for me to give advice. But my advice is based on nearly losing my life. Jesus tells us in John 15:13: *"Greater love has no one than this, that one lay down his life for his friends."*

It comes down to how much you love your neighbor. Are you willing to lay down your life for Him? I don't think most people would physically die for someone else. God knows your heart. And God knows what it means to lay down your life for someone—everyone.

The Apostle Paul says in Romans 5:6–8, *"For while we were still helpless, at the right time Christ died for the ungodly. For one will hardly die for a righteous man; though perhaps for the good man someone would dare even to die. But God demonstrates his own love toward us, in that while we were still sinners, Christ died for us."*

There are many people with many stories about talking to Jesus, demons, or even the devil. You do not know their life. God does know everything, and he works it out for our best. We don't always like the consequences. There are results for our sins. God hates sin, but he loves sinners. What good father doesn't discipline his children? God loves everyone. Even me. I have done some pretty disgusting things in my life. Now, it's not about who did the worst or who did better. God loves you and he knows where you're going. You have a choice. Will you go the right way? I hope so. Only God knows for sure.

God has grown me up little by little. God will never give you more than you can handle.

"No temptation has overtaken you but as such as is common to man; and God is faithful, who will not allow you to be tempted beyond what you are able, but with the temptation will provide the way of escape also, that you may be able to endure it." **1 Corinthians 10:13**.

God doesn't cause consequences for our sins—but by our haste, impatience, or stupidity we may harm ourselves or others. My actions are like everyone else's. They often hurt the people closest to us or the ones we love the most.

CHAPTER 1

Impatience

Mom said I should write on my impatience. I can be very impatient. My mother catches a lot of it.

My impatience is caused by my anger and grief. I have been very impatient my whole life. I wanted to do all and experience everything that looked like it might be fun and exciting.

"There is a way which seems right to a man, But its end is the way of death." **Proverbs 14:12.**

And I was angry if I couldn't do something. The Grief came later.

I was a go-getter from the start, from birth. I wanted to play ball with my older brother and the big boys—and that made me better. One day we were playing football out in the front yard with my brother, his friends, all my uncles, and cousins, and I didn't want to be left out. I surprised everyone that I could play ball with all of them. I could catch the ball, leap like a rabbit, and run like a deer. My talents, skills and attitude spilled over into my success in all my sports: all-state football, basketball, and baseball. But football was my favorite sport. I loved running as fast as I could, and running into people. I was a linebacker and a tailback in high school (I never came off the field) and a free safety in college.

After my fifth game in college—when I was a freshman (I started as a freshman)—I was in my first wreck. It was my car, but I wasn't driving. I was passed out.

When I woke up in the hospital I was madder than hell: "Let me out of here!" A lot of my friends came to see me.

I thought it was going to be like the TV show M*A*S*H*, they would strap me to the outside of the Helicopter and fly me to the hospital, but they took me inside the helicopter. I remember little, but I remember the emergency room and the doctors and nurses surrounding me. But this book is not about that wreck.

You can get a sense of my confused priorities from my attitude in the hospital. Instead of being concerned about the other person in the wreck—or even my own condition—the main thing I was worried about was keeping my four girlfriends separated from each other when they came to see me. I wanted to keep them all. When my mother came to the hospital I begged her to help me keep them from each other. As all women would not, she did not approve of what I had done (or what I intended to do). You must remember, though, I was injured badly, in the hospital, and she loved me. So she helped me.

Before that I had several close calls (went in the ditch, hit the house and bent the drain pipe, and some incidents where I woke up while I was driving), but I don't remember most of them. We all laugh about incidents that occur while we were in a drunken stupor.

It is no longer funny after you have killed someone, but that was in the later wreck, and that time I was driving. It wasn't funny anymore. I think about Rob's death every day.

Some of my aggressive, or even devil-may care attitude, may be seen in my competitive nature, even from earliest childhood. I always strove to play ball with the older boys. And then I was an older boy. When I got to alcohol and drugs the same thing happened. The biggest problem there was I also got to the point where I could outdo the "big boys"— using or selling. It wasn't their fault. I take all the responsibility and blame.

I have been asked what I have been angry about. I am an overachiever. I have to be the best at whatever I am doing.

That has subsided now, a little bit. I always wanted to be the top at everything. I thought that since I found God my anger would go away, but it hasn't. I want to be the best evangelist there is. I have to remember that it is not about me, but about what can be done for the kingdom. That is what is really important in life.

Then I am asked about grief. What grief? Grief is a miserable thing. You can have grief from not having enough or from having too much. Either way, God loves you. He is long-suffering, patient and kind (in fact, all the things I have difficulty with, maybe what we all have difficulty with). That is the advantage He has over us: He is not going anywhere.

Now I understand that God has a special purpose and mission for my being alive. World, you've been warned.

Here I come.

CHAPTER 2

Superman: Becoming a Jesus Freak

Becoming a Jesus Freak was the best move I have ever made. But it did not happen without a trial or without temptation. In my first book I gave the story of how my drinking and drugging led to the serious wreck that turned my life around. But I changed. I had to be changed. I had to turn away from sin and temptation. And I have spoken to the devil in many forms. The devil is Satan.

I have spoken to the Devil, once through a woman I met when I used to mall-walk every day. I used my left index finger to say, "Come here." She began walking toward me, and all I could think was, "Hubba-hubba."

She was a woman I saw every day for eight months. Then, while I was seeing her, another man proposed to her. I told her she better take that relationship, because I am on a mission from God. Perhaps both of them were ditzy. Maybe here "Ditzy" means *Devil.*

I may have been on a mission from God, but I loved her. And I loved her enough to let her go. I had already screwed her up enough the way it was. But she was beautiful, and I loved her. I spoke to the devil through her. I knew better than to do anything with her, but I had in my mind that it was all right. Today I am reminded of John 8:7: *But when they persisted in asking him, he straightened up and said to them, "He who is without sin among you, let him be the first to throw a stone at her."*

I was torn between wanting her and wanting to do the will of God, of deciding if it was love or lust and then deciding to try to do the will of God.

One demon was a guy at college in 1994 who confronted me and shouted, "I hate you!" I think he said this because he wanted to be heard, and because I was disabled and people loved me and were listening to me because I was preaching Jesus. It could be that he may have felt the way he did because he probably hated Jesus and he could not have known my love for everyone, that I do not hate people.

"I hate you," he said again.

I said, "That's OK. We all have our choice in life. Mine is, I love you."

A whole group of people surrounded us, and started clapping, when I said, "I love you."

I said to him, "Jesus loves you and I love you."

Then he looked me in the eye and said a third time, "I hate you."

"That's OK," I said. "We all make choices. My choice is that I love you." The crowd started clapping, so I yelled, "Quit it! Don't you see he feels bad enough?"

They stopped.

Then we went our separate ways. I saw him a couple of days later, walking to class. We talked awhile, and he accepted Jesus through me.

God the Father is so awesome. He loves everyone. I feel this whole event happened for his glory, so that another soul may be brought to heaven.

When you turn to Christ, the devil will be hotter on your tail than ever before. Once you accept Christ, hopefully you will become a threat to the devil and all his demons.

The devil plays for real. He is not a cute little character in a red jump suit carrying a three-pronged pitchfork. The devil can shoot arrows; but he does not have control over your mind—you do. He wants to lie, kill, destroy, and ruin you. He hates you. He hates me. I hate him.

I know we have the victory through Jesus Christ our Lord and Savior. After all, that is why he died for us, so that we may spend eternity with Him. This whole life on earth is meaningless. This only has meaning when we find God's purpose for our life. We are not living for this life; we are living for an eternity with God, Jesus, the Holy Spirit, and all the angels in heaven. I hope to see you all in heaven with me.

CHAPTER 3

The Call

I'm not perfect, but I'm perfectly willing to do God's will.

I have been waiting for this call for quite awhile. Life has been a journey—full of excitement, as I always say, some good, some bad. I know God is completely in control, and if I get out of the way, it will go much better.

What this book shows, most of all what I want you to understand, is that if you screw up, run to Jesus. I'll say it again. **If you screw up, run to Jesus.**

I have a very good story which God has given me. I keep screwing up. And every time anyone screws up, they should run to Jesus. God's grace is greater than all our sins. As Paul says, *"What shall we say then? Are we to continue in sin so that grace may increase? May it never be! How shall we who died to sin still live in it?"* **Romans 6:1–2**.

Or I also consider what else Paul says to me, *"Wretched man that I am! Who will set me free from the body of this death? Thanks be to God through Jesus Christ our Lord! So then, on the one hand I myself with my mind am serving the law of God, but on the other, with my flesh the law of sin."* **Romans 7:24–25**.

No matter how sincerely we want to be perfect, we will screw up in these earth-suits. It is not this world we are living for.

I know where I am going now, but I don't know which road I'll take. I know my destination. All I know is that God loves me, and he is in control.

"And this is his commandment, that we believe in the name of his Son Jesus Christ, and love one another, just as he commanded us." **1 John 3:23.**

I have my own free will, and that is where I get in trouble. It amazes me: everyone else knows just what I should do. And usually they are trying to help. I think to myself, already done that, and I want to *tell* them what to do, but that wouldn't be very Christian like. *"I am crucified with Christ; therefore, I no longer live, but Jesus Christ now lives in me. I have been crucified with Christ; and it is no longer I who live, but Christ lives in me; and the life which I now live in the flesh I live by faith in the Son of God, who loved me and gave Himself up for me."* **Galatians 2:20**

I can quote scripture all I want, but that doesn't mean a whole lot. Only the blood of Jesus is what sets us all free. Consider the words of Jesus: *"You search the Scriptures because you think that in them you have eternal life; it is these that testify about Me; and you are unwilling to come to Me so that you may have life."* **John 5:39–40**

Once, recently, I was in the Qwest Center in Omaha, Nebraska to attend *Promise Keepers*. I tripped and fell and badly hurt my shoulder. God doesn't plan pain or hardship to come on anyone. We bring it on ourselves. I didn't go to the doctor right away; I should have. I have been hurt so many times, I have enough pills that I thought I could get by. But I couldn't. The pills helped me to go to sleep, but when I woke up it hurt worse than before. It wouldn't quit throbbing. I finally went to the hospital 3 hours later. The collar bone was broken, which had been shattered in 2002. (Since my serious wreck in 1989, my left collar bone has been broken four times, my right three times.).

My doctor is Dr. Bodo Treu in Immanuel Hospital in Omaha, Nebraska. He is a strong Christian man, and he's helped me a lot, because I have hurt myself a lot. I don't know what God has planned for me, but I do know that when I met and talked with Jesus, I got my mind blown. So none of this really surprises me. Life is a rat race, but it's not this life we're living for. If you want out of the rat race, run to Jesus.

CHAPTER 4

The Story Continues:
With a New Outlook on Life

I don't want the title to confuse anyone. I thought I was big and bad, but I am nothing without God. I am truly honored and humbled to be a servant of the King, the Lord Jesus Christ. I will go deeper into this later in the book.

I don't want anyone to be confused when I say I met and talked to Jesus. I will also expand on this later in the book.

Believe me, that is a real moment that sticks out in my memory.

There are other moments that really stick out in my memory. Probably one of the biggest was an event at Cunningham Lake in Omaha, Nebraska. I had had a very busy day as usual, was very tired, just wanted to go home and take a nap. The Holy Spirit told me to go to Cunningham Lake; I would be blessed. So I went there. It was February, cold, with a 20 degrees below zero wind chill factor. I had on shorts and a Larry Bird tank top. There was one car out there. So I figured this is whom I'm supposed to talk to. I pulled up beside the car. When I went over, they rolled down the windows, and I could smell marijuana.

I said to them, "Smoking a little wacky tobaccy, huh?" They giggled. I told them I laughed a lot when I was high, but I said, "It is not funny anymore when you kill someone." They said they were sorry. I told them about my book and asked if I could show them one. I told them I used to smoke dope and sell drugs. I thought the drug dealers were my friends. I explained that the drug scene is a downward spiral. You end up needing more and more to get that same feeling back you had when you first got high off pot (it is a tolerance build-up with any drug). Once you are addicted, all you want is your next and better high. Drug dealers know this and prey on people for this reason. I know, because I was a drug dealer. I've had drug deals go bad, cops called on me, guns pulled on me. I didn't care. All I wanted was my next high.

It is a miserable life. Dealers don't care; all they want is your money. Before I knew it, I couldn't stop. I was addicted. (No one ever says, "I want to be an addict.") Don't start, and you'll never miss it. God will always give you a way of escape. Jesus (God) is worth it. In my case, this was not easy. Yet it can be as easy as ABC: Admit, Believe, and Confess. But this life is temporary. It is not this life we are living for. Just Admit. Believe. Confess.

I can only imagine what the people in the car were thinking at how funny it must have been to see me standing in the cold in my tank top and shorts, trying to sell them a book in the middle of nowhere.

They had to think I was crazy, but they all dug into their pockets and came up with $4.35, and said, "This is all we have. Can we have a book?"

I said, "Sure." It really moved me.

Now I will explain what the title of this book refers to. Superman is dead and buried, never to return, but he still pops up every now and then. The story continues in my life, but I no longer desire to be a teacher and coach. I want to see as many people come to Christ as I can. A real burning desire for lost souls and people burns inside of me. God has blessed me, even to the point of being alive. It really hurts me to see people acting just as I did; however, I do not condemn anyone, because the *Bible* says, *"Do not judge, and you will not be judged; and do not condemn, and you will not be condemned; pardon, and you will be pardoned."* **Luke 6:37**

It is similar in Matthew: *"Do not judge, so that you will not be judged." Matthew 7:1*

I had to kill someone before I woke up. No one should have to feel the deep hurt I do when I think about killing someone, the deceased Robert Thomas, every day. What made it hurt all the more is that Rob was a good friend of mine, and the best friend of my brother.

I know God has forgiven me, after all he has done, is doing, and will do for me.

The *Bible* says, *"And it shall be that everyone who calls on the name of the Lord will be saved." Acts 2:21.*

I have become a real learner of the *Bible*. I have read the *Bible* over fifty times. Just for your information, one simple way to remember how many books are in the *Bible* is by remembering one number. The Number is 3. How many books are in the Old Testament? 3 and (3 squared) = 39: 39 books in the Old Testament. 3 x 9 = 27: 27 books in the New Testament. 39 + 27 = 66: 66 books in the *Bible*. We're on Route 66 to Heaven. If you know and submit to the Lord Jesus Christ—He gave his life on that hill at Calvary nearly 2000 years ago—you will receive eternal life.

"…if you confess with your mouth Jesus as Lord and believe in your heart that God raised Him from the dead, you shall be saved; for with the heart man believes, resulting in righteousness, and with the mouth he confesses, resulting in salvation. For the Scripture says, "Whoever believes in Him will not be disappointed." Romans 10:9–12

Now there is so much I want to tell you and show you about the *Bible*, but my best advice to you is to pick up the *Bible*, and read it for yourself. It is the best book ever written or ever will be written.

God is everything. We are all nothing without Him, but Philippians 4:13 says it all: *"I can do all things through Him who strengthens me."*

My favorite verse in the *Bible* is my personal verse. My overhead reading lamp blinked seven times when I read 1 Corinthians 15:10, which says, *"But by the grace of God I am what I am, and his grace toward me did not prove vain; but I labored even more than all of them, yet not I, but the grace of God with me."* I say that verse every morning. I do submit to God. I will do my best, pray that it is blessed, and let God take care of the rest.

The *Bible* is the best book, but you can pick up some words of wisdom from other books too. I'll let the *Bible* explain itself in Psalm 12: *"The promises of the Lord are promises that are pure, silver refined in a furnace on the ground, purified seven times."* **Psalm 12:6**

Today I have a new outlook on life that came from growth since my terrible accident. This growth is not just my experience. I have been a seeker, and I have read and read and read the *Bible*. I have belonged to many churches and I have talked with many pastors. Slowly I have learned to listen—to listen for wisdom here, and, often in the night, to listen for the voice of God. I will say more about that in Chapter 9. I have also learned to listen to the people who care for me. I will talk about that now.

My mother has to be acknowledged and praised a lot. She has been through many trying times with me. Behind every good man is a good woman. Right now I want a wife, but until then, I'll settle for my mother. I hope my wife is like my mother.

I have taken many trips with her and done a lot of speeches with her. We really are best friends. Don't be fooled though. We do argue and fight. We love to play cards together, mainly pitch. And I don't care what she says, I had low. Only the people who play pitch will get that joke.

No matter how much I travel, one of my favorite places will always be Orlando, Florida. The temperature is very nice down there—in the winter 60 to 70 degrees. I love to go to

Orlando because it is the number one vacation spot in the world: there are always people of all races and from all countries.

There are a lot of memories that stick out in my mind. The biggest is when I accepted Jesus, February 19, 1991, in Independence, Missouri, at Independence Regional Hospital, in the chapel, from Bob Zerr, about 12:30. Not that it was important to me or anything: it was the most important moment in my life.

Since the writing of my last book, all my grandparents have died. A very touching moment for me was when my mom's dad, my grandfather, asked me if he could accept Christ from me and be 100% sure that he was going to heaven. I believe he was already going to heaven and a Christian, but it really moved me. It made me cry. I loved him so much, and I know he's in heaven, and I will see him again.

CHAPTER 5

Changes

Whether you like change or not, it is going to happen. Life is a journey. Enjoy the ride. You only get one chance in this life and it is not this life we are living for. God loves change.

When you get too comfortable, get ready for a shake-up to occur. I was just cruising along, everything was going great, and I had an old habit jump up and bite me in the butt. I know I used to be a compulsive gambler, but I couldn't stay away from the casino until I lost $10,000. You always hear about it when someone wins money at the casino. Never do they mention when they lose. The casinos are in business ultimately to take your money, or they wouldn't *be* in business. They are not there to lose money.

Casinos are completely evil. I was playing blackjack for $400.00 a hand. I'm sorry, that is insanity.

On the other hand, a good thing happened through all of this: by a funny series of events I got off pain pills. One night at the casino I was standing beside a 21-year-old wearing a miniskirt, tank top, and no bra. She said to me, "I need a man tonight. You're kinda' cute."

I said, "I'm married. I love God more than hanky panky."

She said, "That's honorable."

Being honorable, I went to the ATM and got another $1,000.00, which I proceeded to lose. Then I left.

I went home at 2:30 AM and read the *Bible*. I had nowhere else to go. Then I prayed. It is a God thing: my shoulder quit hurting as bad. I got off pain pills (during that time I had taken over 800 Darvocet). I can now raise my arm above my head. I had to take pain pills because I was in so much pain, at times I wanted to die. That was God's way of breaking me.

I no longer gamble. I no longer drink. I no longer do drugs. I praise the Lord Jesus Christ with all my heart and soul and mind.

I had a lot of pride and still do. I cannot do everything by myself, but God can. The Triune God (Father, Son, Holy Ghost) was perfectly happy on its own. God created human life in this world—beginning with Adam and Eve. I invite you to read the *Bible* and understand all that has occurred for your own benefit. God will bless you for reading it, and after you read it once, you'll start reading it over again. And again, and again.

This book was written because I was tired of people saying, "What do you do next?"

Well, in answer I say, "Follow God and you'll be all right."

Maybe you have blown it. So what? God loves you. We all blow it every day. Run to Jesus. My main reason for writing this book is to show you from my own life that when you blow it, you can always run to Jesus. God forgives you if you ask Him. *"But where sin increased, grace abounded even more."* **Romans 5:20**

Not my words, but *God's*. Is that exciting, or what? (Read the *Bible*.)

There is more to it than that. *"What shall we say then? Are we to continue in sin so that grace may increase? May it never be! How shall we who died to sin still live in it?"* **Romans 6:1–2.**

All I know for sure is that God loves you. I killed someone (unintentionally), but God forgives me and loves me. This book magnifies God's grace.

"If we confess our sins, he is faithful and just to forgive us our sins and to cleanse us from all unrighteousness." **1John 1:9.**

If you run to God and confess your sins, God will forgive. I know. I live it.

What does the word *Bible* stand for? "**B**asic **I**nstructions **B**efore **L**eaving **E**arth." It is not this world we are living for. Nothing that happens to me surprises me, because on

September 9, 2004, when I met and talked to Jesus, he said, "You are going to get your mind blown." It is happening. It is always my fault when things happen to me that are bad. Thank goodness God will never kick you to the curb when you blow it. I could give you many examples, but we all live our own life. God knows everything and reacts to how we react to the circumstances. The more I know, the more I realize how little I know. My own examples come from my everyday life.

When I think about the word *changes*, it brings back a song I used to listen to quite a bit, by Tom Petty and the Heartbreakers called "Ch-ch-ch-changes." A lot of old songs are brought back to my mind when I am going through life experiences. The same is true of everyone's life. Music is a very strong influence on all of our lives. The first concert I ever went to was in the Civic Auditorium in Omaha, Nebraska, and it was also the first Tom Petty Concert I ever saw. I saw many after that, I kept partying harder and harder. Music had a strong influence on my life and how I acted. We constantly change our minds, thoughts, and the way we live life. One thing never changes in life, and that is God. He knew everything that would happen, everything that has happened, and will happen. Can I explain everything? – No! Can you? What I do know for sure is that God is God. Always has been. Always will be forever and ever.

Things have happened that make some people, whom I highly respect, doubt me. I will never doubt myself. That has always been my strong point in life. I have spoken to the devil twice, three demons, Jesus once. I may be a fool, but I'm not stupid. I feel terrible for what I have put my mother through. God gave me a strong mother because He knew what she would go through. She ain't perfect either, but I am. I am, and we all are, perfect in God's eyes because of what Jesus Christ did for us on that hill of Calvary about 2000 years ago.

Here is my word of advice to everyone: Take time, relax, and enjoy the ride. It will be at times a very bumpy ride.

CHAPTER 6

Churches and Pastors

I am not always an easy person to understand. And I come in conflict with the very people I need and who are trying to help me. Becoming the best evangelist I can be is important to me, and finding a church home is very important to me. But sometimes making all those connections won't work for me.

I have been to several different churches, and I have learned quite a bit from different people everywhere I've been. I have made mistakes, but the problem occurs when people think I'm a robot, and I'm not. Maybe my physical condition makes me look or act like a robot, but I'm not.

I am human. I will make mistakes.

In my search for God (Father, Son, and Holy Spirit), I have made many mistakes. I have been down a rough and winding road. The next part of my story must trace some of that path.

After my second, and worst, wreck, and when I was in my very long rehab at the Independence Regional Health Center, I was helped by the spiritual Chaplain on my floor—Bob Zerr. he wasn't heavy handed, but I was listening mainly for the companionship and because he always brought me junk food I wasn't supposed to have. One day he read from the *Bible* for three and a half hours. For one and a half years he asked me if I wanted to go to the chapel. I would say, "No, but I'll have some junk food."

At this point let me quote from my first book:

I had nowhere else to go but up. I didn't like the position I was in and was willing to do anything to get out of it. I was still determined to walk and to lead a normal life again someday, but I was tired. I knew it was God who had pushed away my thoughts of suicide. And

I had a feeling I had been spared from death in both accidents for a reason other than extreme luck. **Superman Doesn't Live Here Anymore, p.41**

I was not an easy case. However, when he read the *Bible*, I felt myself opening up. When he asked me if I wanted him to stop reading, I said, "No," because I found answers I had been searching for my whole life. My occipital lobe was badly injured in my second wreck. When my eyes wouldn't focus to let me read anything else, I could read the *Bible*.

Again I will quote from my first book:

I went to the chapel every chance I could after that. I never grew tired of hearing someone read from the Bible and later of reading it myself. I found answers to questions I had thought about many times at Rebound. I understood what had happened to me and why. I discovered that being born again means being figuratively reborn for yourself as well as for God. **Superman Doesn't Live Here Anymore, p.42**

When I finally came home, I went to Church with my mother, the old St. John's Missouri Synod Lutheran Church where I went to Sunday School when I was a child. I went there from grade school through confirmation. Typically, I never memorized things before confirmation class, but I was a quick study, and could always say it by heart before I left. That was how I passed. Then I would forget it.

I had quit going to church after confirmation and partied, partied, partied. I partied to fill a void in my heart. I ran away from a God I could not see to booze and drugs and sex which I could see—and feel.

I do not want it to sound like I am attacking the Lutheran church—or any of these churches or pastors—I am simply recounting the tortured journey I have had to faith. I am the problem, and I made many improper or ineffective or downright wrong choices.

For example, in 1995 I began going to Christ Community Church in Omaha. Why? Because my girlfriend went there.

The Pastor, Bob Thune was a great mentor, a class act. But I left that church. Why? Because when he had been gone two weeks on a church trip, one of the assistant pastors—who is no longer there—dismissed me. I was accused of something I didn't do.

Then I went to Trinity Church in Omaha, but I butted heads with the pastor because there were lots of pretty girls in his church. Next it was Westside Community Church in West Omaha, Tony Lambrant, who is now in Louisiana, was there. I really liked him because he was very down to earth, and I could relate to him. Besides, he rode a Harley!

Next I attended the Bellevue, Nebraska Christian Center where Gary Hoyt was another pastor I butted heads with. That was the first church where I took my friend David (who is writing this book). After that I got tired of the "Mega" churches.

Then I went to First Christian in Council Bluffs, Iowa, but, as usual, things happened. I tried Broadway Methodist in Council Bluffs, but I just left after two weeks. Next it was United Baptist in Council Bluffs, and then First Presbyterian.

Finally, it might have seemed that I found a home: I went to Crossroads Christian Center in Council Bluffs, Iowa for over two years. Pastor Brown was not only my pastor, but he became a confidant and dear friend. I know when I left there he didn't want me to leave, but I fully understand why I had to leave. I can understand that my words and actions might have been in conflict with his mission. He had to protect his flock. I love him no matter what happens.

I have sometimes returned to Westside Community Church in Omaha—and I do, because they have great plays at Christmas and Easter, but other forces caused me to seek and find and stay where I am now: the Life Fellowship (non-denominational) Church.

Meanwhile, I had gone to a "challenged" church, special services, thinking I would bless them (They are a church for the handicapped.) They mentally knocked my socks off (First

Presbyterian Church in Council Bluffs, Iowa, at 7:00 on Tuesday evenings in the upper room of a building next door.) I have to accept that I can learn from many churches, that my opinion of what they are is not where they are.

I thought I was so godly. That church showed me innocent faith at work, what getting back to the basics is all about. Innocent faith is a neat thing. When the world gets to us, we try to analyze everything. All you need to know is that God loves you. This was a Tuesday night service for mentally challenged people. It was neat. I got a lot out of it, but I moved on.

One night I had prayed from 10:00 P.M. to 4:00 A.M., seeking the will of God.

I didn't freak out, but wondered where I would go. The answer showed up on my doorstep; there was a knock on the door. I opened the door, knew him, end of story. But the story goes on. I'm spreading my love to as many people as I can.

Well, as I said, it was 4:00 A.M. and I was praying and wondering where I would go, and at 8:00 A.M. the next morning, Frank Farwell, a Pastor at the church I am going to now (and who is a good friend of mine—and who has always been a good friend of mine) was at my door knocking. He asked me, "Are you ready to come to my church yet?"

I said, "Yes."

I love them all so much—the people in this church. I look forward to seeing them all every week. Some of them I also see on Wednesday night.

Obviously, I have had a long and confused search for a church home. Now, however, it has not been my refusal to try; instead it has been my attempt to find a match for me. It is certainly not a matter of God, Christ, and the Holy Spirit. I have been pursuing the faith for over fifteen consecutive years. It is a matter of growing as I need to grow.

Like I said, I love them all so much.

CHAPTER 7

Marriage Partner

Marriage is one of the things I am 100% human about. I would like to be married, as other single people probably feel. When I look at it realistically, I am living a great life now. When I do get married—because I want to—it will be hard to find time like I do now, every day with God. I am usually relaxed and carefree. Don't get me wrong. I blow up, I am human. But you can say, though, that I am a child of the King, and he loves me. That should be enough, but I want more.

I don't listen to God and other people until something bad happens and slows me down. It makes me stop and smell the roses. Often it says, "Hey, knucklehead, slow down. You're screwing up and headed for trouble."

I am getting wiser, though. Car wrecks are not fun. At this time I am trying to finish my second book—this book—and hope that people will be really eager for it. I am trying to write every day, knowing that this might be a problem if I were married. But I want to hurry up, get married, have some children, love God together, and the rest will be history.

That is what I want—getting married and loving God together with a loving spouse—wouldn't everyone want that?

The question that I need to address—that I need to keep asking myself, as all of us do—is "What does God want?"

Ever since I was young, in the first grade, I had two girlfriends at once, and I thought I was the man, because I kissed them. Then in second grade I had only one girlfriend, who turned out to be my cousin. Then in third grade I had a real crush on my teacher. In fourth grade we moved from

Beebeetown to Tri-Center (actually four towns in Iowa: Neola, Persia, Beebeetown, and Minden) where I had a crush on a cute blonde. In fifth grade it was a crush on a girl who later ended up marrying a good friend of mine. There was another for a week.

In the sixth grade a new girl moved in (all mine). It is in sixth grade you notice that the girls are starting to change, and you are really fascinated with that. In the seventh grade I had the hots for an *old* girlfriend, but it didn't last. In the eighth grade I just concentrated on school and sports.

However, in the ninth grade I fell in love big time. I went with her for three and a half years, but broke up with her my senior year to go with a model.

In the thirteenth grade I went to the college where, as we have previously seen in Chapter 5, I had four girlfriends—safely all in different towns. That's what I thought. All my fellow football players thought I was the man. I thought so too. This worked until my first wreck. Women in college helped feed my ego. They used to call me the "Energizer Bunny."

My mother has a different view of these stories.

I was definitely living life—for *me.*

Now I am trying to live my life for *Jesus.*

I wanted to live my life like a movie star. People get all excited in this world over Hollywood stars and people on TV. They cannot give you eternal life. I love them, but they are only people. I love God more than the movie stars and athletes. I'm heaven-bound and will be found by the Lord Jesus Christ who gave his life for all of our sins. Don't we owe Him something?

Enjoy life when you are young—not too much. The older you get, the more all your stupidity as a youth comes out. You start to feel all the aches and pains. In my case, my body is a constant reminder of my own needless suffering.

As I said I was definitely living life—for *me.*

Now I am living life for *Jesus.*

CHAPTER 8

Mind Overload

I am no different from any other human alive. Sometimes my mind races ahead with all the things I think I am going to do. We're all different—or think we're different—and feel we're stretched to the limit. And this may be the point: we want to be the same, want to be different, want to keep going, feel we're stretched to the limit: and only God knows how far each person can go.

Everything you do, everything that happens, comes back to God. And it's a very comforting feeling knowing He is in control, and not me. I screw up every day. It is also comforting to know the *Bible*, and it says, *"but where sin increased, grace abounded all the more." **Romans 5:20.***

I sure can preach well, but when I have to eat my own medicine, it is as bitter as wormwood. If my faith is so great, why am I taking nerve pills to go to sleep? My mind has been racing lately.

February 11, 2006, 10:30 PM: It's another one of those nights. My mind is racing and whirling and whirling. I looked through my book notes and papers—what I have so far, and I wanted to write more on this chapter: "Mind Overload." *One big problem: I couldn't find it (the chapter). I hope David has it. That is just a little of what goes on while writing a book. It doesn't just magically happen. I have been kind of freaking out and praying. It's no one's fault but my own. The old Scott is trying to rear his ugly head again. I rebuke the devil and all his ways. I know I'll be all right because God is the one in control, not me. I have screwed things up all my life. God is more than able to make me what he wants me to be.*

The dream I had keeps coming back to my mind. I am an example for the world, good or bad. It is my choice.

I want people to be encouraged to believe and trust God by my experiences. You probably have not been through all that I have, but if God can take care of me, he surely can take care of you. I'm grateful for the efforts of my writer, David Hufford, and my mother.

CHAPTER 9

Middle-of-the-Night Talks or "I Prayed for Over Five Years"

When God wants to talk, you had better listen. On May 29, 2005, from 2:00 A.M. to 4:00 A.M., God told me, "Let's talk."

I went out on the patio and God said, "I have had everything under control since I formed the universe. Chill out." Nothing has taken me by surprise. He has me right where he knew I would be. I have failed Him over and over, but he will never fail me. He is God; he is my best friend. Everything is a lot better. I am now feeling very confident. High confidence has always been a big part of my life. I was a very cocky athlete, but my cockiness is in the Lord. As Paul says, so that, just as it is written, *"Let him who boasts, boast in the Lord." **1 Corinthians 1:31.***

This is another one of those nights. I'm tired, but I can't go to sleep because my mind is racing. I already got up three times and wrote note cards and finally said, "Ok Lord, I will write."

I want to explain that God is three persons in one. God is a spirit. *"God is spirit, and those who worship Him must worship in spirit and truth." **John 4:24***

Here is the information that the Holy Spirit had me write. There is a lot more information. Read the *Bible* and discover just how much God loves you. There is much more. I know people will say, "You should have written this—or that." My reply is: "Write your own book." This is just my story, and I'm sticking to it.

First, God is God the Father who is ultimately in control of everything, but keeps his hands off and will let us make our own mistakes with our own free will—or it wouldn't be free will. God is loving, merciful, patient, and kind. Most importantly, God is love. We are created in the image of God. We continue to screw it up, but God's grace is greater than all our sins. We all need to run to Jesus.

Second, the second part of the Trinity, is God the Son, Jesus Christ our Savior and the best friend we will ever have. Being able to see the future and the sins we would commit, he died for us anyway. That is how much he loves us. I prayed every day for over 5 years to meet Jesus. I have met Him face to face and talked to Him for twenty-five minutes on September 9, 2004, in Heartland of America Park in Omaha, Nebraska, at 8:05 P.M. He is the best friend you will ever have. He died for all of your sins. He is the mediator between you—anyone—and God.

Third, God is the Holy Spirit. He is that subconscious thought in your mind that tells you what you should or shouldn't do. Again, he won't force himself on anyone, or it wouldn't be free will. A lot of times people think and say, "Where did that thought come from?" The Holy Spirit is trying to nudge you in the right direction. Everyone has his own choice, what he should do, and which way he should go. The Holy Spirit will never lie to you.

Since things are going so well for me, why am I feeling so bad? We all have these moments in our lives. I've had a good day, but I feel rotten. Don't you dare say it! OK, I'll admit it: *I'm human, and that's what scares me—maybe it scares all of us at times.*

Who is the Devil? In Chapter 2 I tried to express my encounters with Satan as how I acted in my encounters with other people. The Devil is the Prince of Darkness, the Father of lies, also referred to as Satan. (That power of darkness can make me think something wrong—even something wrong about you. Also in Chapter 2 I tried to show how that affected me in terms of others and others in terms of me.) Satan is completely an evil spirit. There is no good in him. He is the father of lies. *"You are of your father the devil, and you want to do the desires of your father. He was a murderer from the beginning, and does not stand in the truth because there is no truth in him. Whenever he speaks a lie, he speaks from his own nature, for he is a liar and the father of lies."* **John 8:44**

This is all information that God (the Holy Spirit) told me to write.

One thing he knows and that I have to remember is that Satan was created by God, and he must submit to God. When he was the top angel in Heaven, his name was Lucifer. He wanted to be equal in power to God. Being the top angel wasn't enough. He rebelled and was kicked out of Heaven and thrown into the Lake of Fire or darkness (which is also called Hell), as we know it. His demons also went to Hell with him. Christ explained that in Luke 10:18 when he says, *"I was watching Satan fall from heaven like lightning."*

One thing you must remember, the devil is stronger than we humans are, but he is not stronger than God the Father. So when you screw up, run to Jesus. Repent.

The Devil is after everyone. He hates you; he hates me. I hate him so bad. All you have to do is run to the Father and confess your sins, resist the devil, and he must flee from you. *"Submit therefore to God. Resist the devil and he will flee from you."* **James 4:7**

Satan often works best when we are tired. He loves to kick you when you're down. He has no remorseful feelings at all. He wants to blame the world for being kicked out of heaven and thrown into the lake of fire (hell). You need to constantly refresh your mind and body to withstand the darts of the evil one.

Naps are good for any person. It refreshes you and lets your mind think more clearly. Jesus withdrew to be alone and rest. One story from Matthew tells how he was asleep on the boat during a terrible storm, and he was awakened by his disciples (Matthew 8:23–27). We all need to get a rest.

Injured people may need more rest. Head injured people may need more still.

We all need rest and to refresh ourselves. The problem for me is that I have been head injured—twice—and I am still trying to continue in my traditional ways. All of my life I have defied the odds. I needed (and still need) the sleep of head-injured people, but I defy what is typical of head-injured people and would sleep only five or six hours a night. That is my rebellion coming out. Even today I should be sleeping a lot more. Yet it is at the times I awaken that I have my middle-of-the-night talks with God. That is, it may be rebelliousness; it may be my attempt to answer God.

It has been said that dying was the most he could do for us; the least we can do is live for Him:

"...present your bodies as a living and holy sacrifice, acceptable to God..." **Romans 12:1**

If losing a little sleep is a way I can live for Him, then I'll lose some sleep. I wouldn't want to miss my middle-of-the-night talk with God.

CHAPTER 10

An Event on September 9, 2004

On an early evening, September 9, 2004, while I was at home in Honey Creek, Iowa, I received a message from the Holy Spirit. I was told to go to the Heartland of America Park in Omaha, Nebraska.

"Do you want me to meet Jesus?" I asked, sarcastically.

"Yes," was the only answer.

I was very tired. I finally had a full day off, but I got in my car and went to Heartland Park, about a twenty mile drive from my home. It is a popular place for people to go for a walk, and also where kids hang out. So I often go there to do my work and sell my books.

About sundown, at 8:05 P.M. under a 75% cloudy sky, I looked at the radio clock in the car. I didn't understand at the time, but I remember wondering about why 8:05 was important. Now I know.

As I walked around Heartland Park, I saw a clean cut man sitting on a bench. I approached Him sitting under the overhang. The first thing I noticed was his brown leather hat, with a round rim. He wore a brown and white checked square shirt and gray trousers.

"Like my hat?" I asked.

He said, "You have a nice hat."

I said, "Thank you, but I know that." But mine was black leather.

I touched the cross on his chest and asked, "What's this?" When he looked down I quickly raised my hand and clipped his nose. (I always do something like this; it is kind of a bad trick I play.) I know he knew what I was doing, but he looked anyway, to amuse me. That is how good Jesus is. Again I noticed how very clean cut he was, and from what I could see from beneath the round brim of his hat, his hair was neatly combed. I saw he wore a pair of light tan loafers, and I found it remarkable that he wore no socks. But then I wasn't wearing any socks, either.

Suddenly I had to go to the bathroom. I said to myself, if this is Jesus, he'll be there when I get back. I went to the bathroom, and when I came back he was still sitting there. So I joined Him on the bench.

We sat on the wooden bench under the overhang by the lake. I offered Him one of my books, and he said, "I know what it says." Then he added, Rabboni is happy, very happy, with you." People were walking by as we sat on the bench.

We stood up and were talking by the lake. I remember that I had my arm against a pole. He asked, "Do you want your hands healed?"

I said, "No, God will do that."

He said, "I am." That was when light bulb #1 went off, because I was still questioning in the back of my mind. I didn't fully comprehend.

I never thought about it then, but I could have asked Him if I could walk on water.

He prayed over my right shoulder and said, "Meshiki, Meshiki." ("Father. Father.")

Finally I said to Him, "I have really enjoyed our time together. Thank you for answering my prayer. I prayed every day for over five years for this moment. I know you are a very busy man; you have the whole world to look after. It honors me that you came down and spoke to me."

He said to me, "You are going to get your mind blown."

I didn't know how to respond. It was 8:30 P.M. The entire exchange had been less than a half an hour.

Now that I have met and talked to Jesus, *Bring it on world! NO FEAR HERE.*

I had glanced at the clock in the car and it read 8:05. I didn't know why at the time, but now I do.

I had told Him that I wanted to change my life.

Jesus said, "That is why I died for everyone's sins."

In my opinion, are my mistakes right? No, but that is why Jesus died for our sins. Sin has a trickle-down effect. What I say or think doesn't really matter. I am not God. If you continue in sin, your heart will harden to sin.

Romans 8:1 tells us, *"There is now no condemnation for those who are in Christ Jesus."* Run to Jesus. I was so ashamed I didn't tell the whole truth while writing this book, until God told me to tell the truth so that I might help others.

CHAPTER 11

Heartland Revisited

The Heartland of America Park in Omaha Nebraska, where I met Christ, is also where I do much of my missionary work. A couple of instances may illustrate this.

In Heartland Park a drunk guy was cursing Jesus and saying, "F— God!"—he was falling-down drunk.

I said, "You better quit that."

He said, "Why?"

I said, "God loves you and I love you." He cursed God again.

I said, "You asked for it," and laid my hands on him and started praying over him. He instantly calmed down—he got sober—and said, "I believe. How do I get God in my life?"

I asked him if he wanted to accept Jesus Christ.

He said, "Can you get someone to help me?"

I said, "Better than that, we can go to the Father right now. If you want to accept Jesus Christ into your life, you will receive eternal life." Then I said, I will say the sinner's prayer out loud, and you repeat after me, "…And the *Bible* says *"Whoever calls on the name of the Lord will be saved."* **Romans 10:13**

He did that.

Then we hugged, and I kissed him on the cheek and he kissed me on the cheek.

He was going to his parents' house.

The point is, we don't have to wait for someone who can help.

Another day I had had a very good night selling books at the Heartland of America Park. As I was leaving, I met a couple, broke and down on their luck, as I learned in talking to them. I would have sold them a book, but they said, "We don't have any money; we're poor; we've been laid off."

I asked them if they had had anything to eat lately.

They said, "No,"

I asked them how much would help.

They said, "Ten dollars will be enough."

I offered twenty dollars, but they said ten dollars would be enough, half for food, half for gas.

When I gave them the money, they couldn't understand why I would give it to them.

I just gave them the number of the 36th Street Life Fellowship, the house where I went to church. Now I go to "Life" in Council Bluffs, Iowa, a spin-off from the 36th St. Life Fellowship.

A lot of people I talk with I never see again, but these stories God brought back to me for my book. I never see a lot of people after they accept Christ. That doesn't bother me. I plant; others water, and God gives the increase.

Again the point is, we don't have to wait for someone who can help. That has already happened. *"Whoever will call on the name of the Lord will be saved."* **Romans 10:13.**

CHAPTER 12

My Mom

I was tempted to make this chapter short, something like: "I'm drinking too much pop, and my mother cooks very well. I don't really care. God loves me. End of it.

However, in whatever way it might be like me to say something like that, it would be disrespectful of the one who has given me so much, my mom. I have needed much more from my mother than most. All mothers around the world must be recognized. Mothers are in a league of their own, at least my mother is. Here are just a few of the things she has done for me.

First, she has always believed in me. She believed I would live to come all the way back—not just survive, even when medical opinion was to the contrary. In the second of my two terrible wrecks I was life-flighted to St. Joseph's Hospital in Omaha, Nebraska. I was there 26 days in intensive care, followed by one month of critical care.

After being life-flighted to St. Joe's, I was treated for many serious injuries, among them a deflated left lung and my pelvic bones separated. My pelvic bones had been pushed four or five inches apart from each other. I wore a pelvic apparatus for a long time.

After I was medically stabilized, I was taken from St. Joseph's to Immanuel Hospital for two months of rehabilitation. There the best thing they ever did for me was to tell mom there was no hope for me. The doctor who said that ended up accepting Jesus through me. That was a major turning point for me, because I had no doubt about what God wanted me to do in life: serve Him and spread the good news to as many people as I could.

After I returned from rehab in Kansas City, I approached him while he was sitting at his desk doing paperwork. He had recently seen me speak at St. Joseph's Hospital in Omaha. I spoke at the Neuro-connection for Brain-injured People—for all the doctors and nurses. I wanted to encourage them: there is always hope in Jesus.

But what I was then was not the shattered man I was when they were working on me, the one for whom there had been no hope.

At first they could judge my condition only if I blinked. One of my nurses at Immanuel—Christie Barnes from Missouri Valley, Iowa—told my mother within my hearing that Missouri Valley's team was better than Tri Center. I would blink my eyes for "no," but the therapists wouldn't accept it because I wouldn't do it on a consistent basis. Truth be known, I felt the therapists were insulting me: they would hold a pencil and ask me if it was a pencil, by blinking once for yes, twice for no. I would just close my eyes and go to sleep. At the time that was the only way I could show my displeasure at their insulting my intelligence. I am sure then, just as I sometimes get treated today, that some people think I am stupid because of how I walk and talk. I am a very intelligent person—just ask me.

Throughout all of my medical suffering, my mother did not give up on me.

Let me clarify what she was going through during the times I was mainly in a stage 1 coma. (There are 9 stages to a coma. I went through them all.) First was the wreck itself, on October 10, 1989, followed by 26 days in intensive care at St. Joseph Hospital, and one month of critical care. That would be painful for any parent. Then I was sent to Immanuel Hospital rehabilitation for two months. My situation was dismal. Then I was sent to Independence, Missouri to the hospital facility called "Rebound," now known as the Kansas City Health and Rehabilitation Network. My mother had to endure numerous 400 mile round trips just to be with me. When I didn't come home it was because of more surgeries and recoveries. And when I could come home on weekends it was an over 800 mile trip for her—every weekend.

At this latter facility Dr. Gregory Hummel did surgeries that doctors at my previous two hospitals wouldn't attempt. He is my Superman on earth. But my mother knew how determined I have been my whole life. She was with me through all of this. She never gave up on me.

That story, the story of my rehabilitation, was the subject of my previous book.

This book is trying to show how the man I used to be is becoming the man Jesus would want me to be. My mother has been part of all that too.

Second, my mother has always taken me where I needed to go when I couldn't drive. For a long time she had to do nearly everything for me. I couldn't even open a can of pop (we started this chapter that way—remember? I drink too much pop). But my mother had to do other things as well: I learned to dress myself, but she had to do my socks. And she had to do what she did for me when I was a baby: I couldn't even wipe my butt.

Third, my mother has always had a plate of food for me—not just junk but three courses of her good home-cooking—ready for me to put in the microwave. She cooks very well, that's one way I know God loves me. Like I said, I could end it there, but why end it there?

Fourth, My mother plays cards with me. This, of course, is probably a test of her patience. I sometimes lose my cool. As we have seen, I lack patience. She still plays cards with me, mainly pitch. That says a lot. (And I always have low.)

Fifth, she washes my clothes and hangs them up for me. And that says a lot.

Sixth, she is proud to have my friends come up and meet her, including my friend who is writing this book, even when he brings his friends. She always makes them feel at home.

Seventh: the house is usually clean, unless her grandchildren—my nieces and nephews—have been here playing and messing things up, which, since it is my mom, is nearly every day.

Eighth, she has her faults, but I love her. After all, it was my mom who had to drive 800 miles every weekend just to bring me home.

A dream and a kiss: April 20, 1989: to conclude the above list, and the horrible sequence that necessitated it, let me reflect on the events immediately preceding my horrible wreck. I had been up longer than I had ever been without eating or sleeping: eight days and seven nights. Fearing my drinking and drugging, I remember I knelt down to pray, "Lord, let me go to sleep, and I'll never do it again." (How many addicts or alcoholics have prayed that prayer?) But God knew I was lying. But I touched his heart. I called upon his name in my distress. That night—or morning—I dreamt that I was an example for the world. I later dreamed about the wreck that occurred six months later.

The day of my wreck, October 10, 1989, as I was leaving in my car, for some unexplainable reason I backed my car back into the driveway, jumped out of my car, ran into the house, and gave my mother a big hug and kiss and said, "I love you; you're the greatest, 'Bye." Those are the last words she heard me say for over a year. But because of my wreck, I remember none of this.

The following story might serve as a postlude for this chapter. It was, in September, 2005, an "out-take" of this book. In late evening in November, 2004, I was walking along the ocean with my mother, in Oceanside, California. We were going to the pier, when we passed six boys, sitting on seats. (My mother has gotten used to what follows.) I turned around, looked at the boys, and said to one of them, "Smoking a little of that 'wacky tobacky'?" (It has a distinct smell.) The one in the middle pointed his thumbs to the ones on each side, and said, "No, they are."

At that point I said, "Let me tell you a story." After telling my story, I left my book with them, with parting remarks that "the choice" was theirs, how they wanted to live their lives.

Later, upon returning to the resort, I did not find the book in the trash, or around the area. It will never be known if they read my book, or if in some way I, through God's help, helped them in some way. The only thing that's known for sure is, it's still hard for my mother to let me go and do my thing.

She is a mom. My mom.

CHAPTER 13

Friends

We are helped on our way by friends. I have many friends, but I would like to talk about two, Doug and Dave.

It was a Sunday, December 27, 2004, when my friend Doug Holiday (my best friend) and I went to South Dakota. We took his six year-old grandson, and we met his daughter's husband with whom we dropped the child off. Then we came back home. It was the best road trip I ever had. We laughed. And we laughed. And we laughed.

Somehow I can talk about anything with Doug. He is 58 years old, and he knows and has experienced a lot about life. I met him in Heartland Park, in Omaha, Nebraska, in March, 1995. I looked into his eyes and the Holy Spirit told me, "Stick close to this man." We have seen each other at least once a week since 1995, and often more than that. We don't meet only when I go on talking tours or vacation. He remains my best friend to this day.

A different kind of friendship exists between me and my friend, Dave Hufford. We have shared different kinds of experiences, but especially those having to do with recovery, with religion—any topic, and this book. He contributed to my last book and is helping me write this one. He is a teacher, but he was not my teacher. He is a Christian, but we disagree on nearly everything. But we are one in the Spirit. He is writing this book, but at that point it is my book, and there isn't any argument.

With Dave and Scott anyone would wish they were a mouse in the corner: they would get an earful. When they are not writing this book they talk about life. And they have both lived interesting and exciting lives.

When I went on my road trip to South Dakota with my best friend Doug Holiday, he told me very deep things about himself I had never heard before. It brought us closer and made me love him even more. I'm sure he doesn't want me to disclose his personal life. He has Jesus in his life now, and he is a very good man. I look up to him and respect him a lot. He is the best friend I've ever had or ever will have on earth. He has a lot of good ideas. He is an entrepreneur.

My friend David Hufford, who is also writing this book for me, and I have really had fun and enjoyed one another's company. I can only handle him for so long and vice-versa. We are two exuberant, God-loving people. We have both done things we shouldn't have, but we know we need to run to Jesus. Dave has helped me immensely in writing this book. We've had a lot of good times, but, as I mentioned in a previous chapter, we disagree on a lot of the minute points.

Recently Dave was whining to me about forgetting the papers he had worked really hard on. I asked him, "Do you want me to call the '*Wambulance?*'" (I got that phrase from my latest special significant other.)

With both of my friends, Doug and Dave, we have a lot of fun, but we also have very deep philosophical discussions about the many women in our lives. Doug is married; Dave has been married—twice. I have never been married.

I hope I will be married to one person only for the rest of my life. I will not get married unless God confirms it.

I will end this chapter as I began it: we are helped on our way by friends.

I have been blessed with many friends.

CHAPTER 14

Jails

What kinds of jails are there? I have a physical jail of my severe handicaps. Some people put themselves in a jail of their own mind—or some other jail of their own making. Some, of course, are sentenced to jail by the court system.

In my mission today I go into jails to speak with the inmates there. The Jail Chaplain, Dick Arant, calls me a "Loose Cannon" because he never knows what I'm going to say or do, and that's good, because I don't know either. "Loose Cannon" is the best description of me I have ever heard. I take his critical comments kindly. They are meant to be helpful.

I have come in contact with many people in jail, a lot of whom are my friends.

There are many good people in the jails who just got caught. Many of us have done just as bad or worse, but we just never got caught. And we laugh when it is really not funny. A lot of the people in jail just need a new chance in life. They are good people with good morals who got caught doing the wrong thing. It is true that many feel remorse only *after* they got caught. *"There is a way which seems right to a man, but its end is the way of death." Proverbs 14:12.*

Today I feel terrible looking back at what I have done. I probably wouldn't have straightened up without my second, serious, wreck. I would have partied all the way to Hell. Now I am heaven bound, on solid ground.

I was asked not to return to the jail because I went in all beebopping and happy with my book in hand. A jail is for people who have made bad choices in life. We all have.

Hopefully, in prison, if that is where you are, you will come to God.

However much I like to see myself as a helpful and busy missionary, my actions are not always the best. I must accept that and try to change. My attitude gets me in trouble, and my mouth gets me in trouble. Sometimes I think I'm doing the work of Jesus; others may see it as Scott doing the funny business of Scott. Sadly, they are sometimes right. Chaplain Dick, mentioned above, had to write me a sharp letter, which I will excerpt here: *"First of all, Scott, you and I have talked frankly about this before, and I thought I had made myself clear, but I am informed that the manner in which you interact with our staff continues to be offensive and inappropriate. We recognize that you do not intend to cause problems, and that you are an unusually outgoing and friendly person....I have discussed this on-going problem with our office staff, and have taken it upon myself to ask you not [sic] to come into our office anymore....I am informing the staff that, as far as I am concerned, you are no longer welcome in this facility...."*
Chaplain Dick Arant

Not to make light of a serious situation, but where they were throwing Saint Paul into jail, they are throwing me out.

Malls have also banned me for preaching and selling my book. I do what I do because I do not want anyone to go to hell.

Please, whatever you do, do not follow me. I will fail you every time. One day I was really feeling my wild oats and I went to an old bar I used to go to all the time. A woman in the bar knew me and instantly began to freak out and oppose me for no reason that was clear to me. I asked her what she was so mad about, why she was opposing me.

She replied, "You know."

People are so upset with me for either what I am trying to accomplish, or they cannot see the progress over time. They only know what I used to be. The very people I want to help oppose me. I have learned I just have to deal with it.

Another woman who opposed me said, "You want your cake and eat it too" (in some respects she could be right). She is married and I want to help her. In reply I said, "Isn't that the pot calling the kettle black?"

Everyone wants to write a book, and you say to yourself, "I'll remember that." You won't. You have to have discipline. You write a book when you have a thought or idea. You have to write it down or you'll forget it. Sin comes back on you. It has a trickle-down effect. The conflict between the good we want to do and sin also imprisons us. And sin is a jail.

"Wretched man that I am! Who will set me free from the body of this death?" **Romans 7:24.**

Most women have more than one pair of shoes. Shoes cost money. There are people starving to death every day. Are those shoes more important than someone's life? You can judge people all you want. Do you not know what God says? *"No one is good, no not one. No one is without sin. For all have sinned and fall short of the glory of God."* **Romans 3:23**.

I know a lot of people will talk smack about me and my book. Don't believe it until you ask me directly and personally.

CHAPTER 15

Where to From Here?

I am not saying I am some holier-than-thou Christian. I am a rotten sinner like every other human being alive. The biggest difference between the old Scott and the new Scott is that I can confess my sins to God and admit when I am wrong. That is something the old Scott could not do.

Now, I realize that I have told you to follow me and not to follow me. The only thing I am 100% sure about is about pointing you to the one who will never fail you.

Everyone has a chance to make a choice in his life that will affect every other choice in his life. Let me rephrase that: there is one choice that is about every other choice you will make. Are you going to accept or reject the Lord Jesus Christ?

He is the one who died for you and your sins.

If you want to go to heaven, here is what you pray to God the Father Almighty: "I confess the fact that I am a miserable and rotten sinner. I know I need a savior to redeem me for all my sins. I believe Jesus Christ gave his life on the hill of Calvary about 2000 years ago. I hate the devil with a passion. Holy Spirit, fall fresh on me and make me what you want, not what I want, but what you want, so that I may bring honor to the Father's name, in Jesus' name, Amen"

It is faith that saves. I am given that faith through grace. It is that faith that humbles me even as it removes my fear. *"For by grace you have been saved through faith and that not of yourselves, it is the gift of God; not as the result of works, that no one should boast." Ephesians 2:8–9*

I used to be a player, but now I'm played—by God. (Oh, I still have to break down sometimes). But what God has done for me just shows how awesome God is. It has been my purpose to show how awesome God has been in my life. It has always been my purpose to tell the world about Jesus Christ. And I have shown how an unholy man can find his way to Jesus.

On my way to Jesus I have often found that I must help others find Jesus, too. By serving others I am actually only serving myself because my overall mission and goal in life is to help other people to find Jesus.

"There is a way which seems right to a man, but its end is the way of death." **Proverbs 14:12.**

I was often going only my own way. I have done some pretty disgusting things in my life. But today I know to run to Jesus.

It is not easy. It really wasn't easy for me. Hopefully by now you have a little better understanding of the road I have journeyed. It is my own fault and choice for the road I have traveled. I can honestly say even after all the pain I've been through, it was worth it all. Why? I found Jesus, and I know I have eternal life. I had to go down every road I did to get here. The road I'm on has a destination: HEAVEN. It is the wildest ride I have ever been on. If you live the Christian life right, it is a lot of fun. Don't beat yourself up when you blow it. Run to Jesus.

We all blow it every day. As you have seen, I need Jesus more than ever. Once you accept Christ, it gives you a reason for living. But the Devil will do whatever he can to get you back. He is the father of lies, and will lie to you all the way. If you want to follow him, you'll be SORRY. Maybe that's it, the last SORRY is the loss of HEAVEN.

God loves you, and I love you. To all who are going to Heaven and the Streets of gold, "May I have this dance?" Well, if you can't dance, you still get the victory. Maybe in heaven everybody can dance. Either way, I know we have the victory through Jesus Christ our Lord and Savior.

CHAPTER 16

Fear Not Only Believe

Fear not; only believe. Those four words mean so much when you have God in your life. You still have hardships and trials, but hopefully you grow a little bit and your fear level will go down, when the devil shoots arrows at you and tells you lies. The deeper you know and fall in love with God, through your faith you will believe and know that God almighty is more than powerful enough to handle every situation that comes your way. Your fear will subside and you will just believe in the One who has complete control if you let Him have it.

What I hope that everyone learned from this book is that when you blow it big time and other people condemn and persecute you, the answer is always: run to Jesus. Does that mean it is OK to sin? No. God forbid, may it never be. We all blow it. All you need to remember is that by grace you have been saved through faith, as it says in Ephesians 2:8, *"...and this is not your own doing, it is the gift of God."* Is that cool, or what? These are not my words, but God almighty. So chill out. Love life, but remember he never sleeps and always has an eye on you.

Everyone says, "No one knows what I go through." God knows, and he promises he will never give you more than you can handle. I used to play games. Now I get played. What goes around, comes around.

I knew there would be people who would oppose me and my book. That's OK. We all have our own thoughts and ideas. We all have different relationships with God.

He loves you. I love you. Put on your seatbelt. Enjoy the ride. I'll meet you in heaven, hopefully—your choice.

I want to praise the Lord Jesus Christ around the world and tell everyone how much he loves them and how powerful he is. No mind can fathom or comprehend God's infinite wisdom and power. As your faith grows deeper, hopefully your fear will begin to subside in your walk in life.

Scott McPhillips

by Gaylord Schelling

Gaylord Schelling was Scott's coach at Tri Center High School in Neola, Iowa. Today, Coach Schelling is at Atlantic High School in Atlantic, Iowa. Coach Schelling contributed the Foreword to Scott's first book, and has graciously offered this testimonial to this book.

January 2006
Scott McPhillips

Scott has been a special person in my life for over 25 years. Scott was a student athlete for me at Tri Center where he played football and baseball.

Scott was a challenge because he loved to live life on the edge. We had many opportunities for counseling sessions as I visited with Scott about his social decisions. I counseled him on both dating and substance abuse. I encouraged him to make decisions which would lead to self-respect and respect for the opposite sex.

One day near the end of his junior year, I took him in the coaching office where I had a heart to heart talk with Scott that got pretty heated. I talked very sternly to Scott about my concerns with his behavior outside of school and how it would affect his personal life and his life as an athlete. Scott knew I was very serious as I presented my concerns to him and asked for a commitment that he would change his activities and behaviors to ones that were more positive.

Scott was the ultimate competitor. If someone said he couldn't do it, Scott would prove the person wrong. There was no challenge or mountain that Scott would not overcome. As a football player, Scott found ways for Tri Center to win. Twice he caught game winning touchdowns against our fiercest rival—Griswold—in the last quarter of play.

Baseball was also a great sport for Scott. He led Tri Center to state runner up and state championship during his junior and senior years of high school. If Scott had not injured his back during his junior year, I believe we would have won back-to-back state championships under his pitching talent. During the state championship game his senior year, Scott hit a two run homerun in the first inning to lead Tri-Center to the championship. Scott thrived on tough or clutch situations— nothing made him work harder than pressure situations. He made plays and willed his team to win.

Scott went on to star at Simpson College playing football as a freshman. Scott still couldn't overcome his worst hurdle, drugs. This led to an accident that changed his life. This accident changed Scott's life, but a friend lost his life that night. When I went to visit Scott in the hospital, I knew his drive would enable him to recover. Scott had a long road even to recover movement. After months and months of rehab, Scott finally came to my home to visit. The doctors said Scott would never walk, talk, or use his hands or arms. Scott proved the doctors wrong on all counts. He can now walk, talk, and even drive a car.

Through his long road to recovery, Scott became a Christian. This brings us to the present day Scott. Scott has spoken to my students about making choices and doing what is right. The lesson that I tried to pass on to Scott in high school is now one he is passing on to high school students. Scott helps me in my teaching and coaching by his example of what choices can do to one's goals in life. Scott is a special young man who beat the odds after a debilitating accident. His mother is one of the reasons Scott is the man he is today. She deserves much of the credit for sticking by Scott and teaching him to never give up when life throws you a curve.

Sincerely,
Gaylord Schelling
Atlantic High School

Painful Lesson
Former Star Athlete Hopes Others Will Learn from His Fatal Mistake

by Tom McMahon

Reprinted by permission from
The Daily Nonpareil, Tuesday, June 7, 2005

HONEY CREEK—On the surface, act one of Scott McPhillips' (then known as Scott Krumwiede) life is every young man's dream.

An all-state athlete at Tri-Center High School, he excelled in baseball, football and basketball and was on a pro football career path. It was 1987.

Act two begins on Oct. 10, 1989. McPhillips, high on drugs and alcohol, is driving down a rural gravel road in a stupor when his car hits another head on. The other driver, his brother's best friend, is killed.

McPhillips begins a nine-month coma. When he emerges, he can't walk or talk, and his body is contorted into a hunched position. His friends abandon him. His dreams of a sports career, along with his body, are shattered.

Act three of McPhillips' life begins Feb. 19, 1991, in an Independence, Mo., hospital chapel—at 12:30 P.M. The spiritual counselor, Bob Zerr, began reading the Bible to him, while McPhillips was still in the midst of his recovery.

"I had no where else to go but up," he said. When Zerr started reading, McPhillips said he felt himself open up. "It felt so good. He read for three and one-half hours."

McPhillips life story is still being written. The 36-year-old now spends his time telling his story—to preschoolers, nursing home residents and all ages in between. He's distributed more than 20,000 copies of his first book, "Superman Doesn't Live Here Anymore," and is working on a second. A companion video tracks the path of an invincible teen to a physically disabled, but spiritually and mentally vibrant man.

"I was a wild little guy," McPhillips laughed, "I was a legend in my own mind." His slowed speech has not slowed his sense of humor.

McPhillips was a big man on the Tri-Center campus.

His head coach, Gaylord Schelling, wrote of him, "(He) was the best athlete I ever coached….Many athletes shy away from pressure plays, but Scott thrived on them. He loved having the ball during crucial game situations….Probably his best quality was that he never quit, no matter what the score was. Scott amazed with his ability to some through with the play to win the game."

But Schelling also became aware of his star athlete's drug problem. While McPhillips listened on the football field, he paid no attention to his coach's admonitions to stop drinking and drugging.

"He was a spiritual freak," McPhillips says of his former coach. "I wasn't. I was a little party boy."

He said he started using marijuana in junior high and soon began drinking.

"I did it all," McPhillips said, "Everything but shoot up. I never stuck a needle in my arm."

McPhillips began supplying drugs to other young people and some not so young.

"I knew a lot of people. I hung around with a lot of older people. I was a big star athlete. People wanted to be with me," he said.

Despite his increasing drug problem, McPhillips excelled in athletics, being named All State in basketball, football, and baseball.

"I remember playing in a football game with a vial of cocaine in my hip pocket. I thought using coke would improve my game. It never dawned on me that some of my best games were played without drugs," he wrote.

His path to fame and fortune got derailed following his first accident, Oct. 22, 1987. McPhillips was a Simpson College freshman and starting cornerback on the school's football team. He and a friend were driving stoned along Interstate 80 when the car hit a guardrail.

He sustained a broken arm and head injury that ended his football career. McPhillips quickly lost interest in school and left Simpson, returning home to Honey Creek, with plans to enroll at Iowa Western Community College and play baseball.

"I started classes during the 1988–89 term, but true to form, I concentrated on fun and games rather than getting a degree. McPhillips failed every class and had an uneventful baseball season.

His downward spiral finally hit bottom following the October 1989 accident when McPhillips says he fell off the top of the world. His mother, Bev Krumwiede, who now does presentations with her son, said her son left his job and went to the bar that evening where he consumed 10 shots of Jack Daniels.

"He stumbled out of the place, but a friend brought him back for another," she said. Krumwiede said her son's blood alcohol level was 2.4 four hours following the accident.

The coma, several surgeries and extensive rehabilitation followed. Doctors had to lengthen his legs and surgically uncurl his hands that had been locked in clenched position during the coma.

"He couldn't talk for over a year," Krumwiede said. Although McPhillips has made great progress, one must pay attention to understand him. "I think God didn't bring his speech back 100 percent so that the kids will have to listen when he talks," Krumwiede said. And talking is a big part of McPhillips' life today.

"I have done over 150 presentations," he said. "Sometimes my mom goes with me and sometimes I do them alone," he said.

McPhillips recalls visiting with an 88-year-old nursing home resident who accepted Jesus when they talked.

"He passed away a week later," he said.

Then there was the little girl in the wheelchair. McPhillips made a fuss over her, telling her she was special and that he loved her. Krumwiede said the school staff told her it was the happiest they had ever seen her.

"I know how much it can hurt to be in a wheelchair, to be different," McPhillips said. "I was used to the physical pain, and I kind of even liked it," he said. "It made me a great athlete. But the mental part—people making fun of me—that hurt."

But the pain is all part of God's plan, McPhillips said.

"God has a plan, and I will follow it," he said.

McPhillips and his mother have several messages they sent to listeners: Realize the dangers of drugs and alcohol, discover how faith in God can help heal body and soul, rediscover your values and what is important in life, appreciate good physical and mental health and retain a positive attitude while overcoming physical and emotional challenges.

"I don't want to preach. I want to tell my story....I hope if young people can identify with me, they might vicariously share even a little of my experience and get the message. It's a lot easier to learn from seeing someone else burn their fingers on a hot stove than to do it yourself," McPhillips said.

Faith is a key element in both their lives. Both had spiritual experiences during McPhillips' recovery.

"I spent a lot of time thinking while I was driving back and forth from the hospital," his mother said. McPhillips was in Independence, Mo, and Krumwiede made the I-29 trek weekly.

"One day while I was in the car I felt a cool mist inside the car and heard a voice say everything was going to be OK," she said.

McPhillips recalls Sept. 9, 2004, when he was at Heartland of America Park in Omaha. "I met and talked with Jesus Christ," he said. It was an answer to a five-year prayer and confirmed an already strong faith.

"I am trying to make a difference," McPhillips said. "Not for my glory—I'm over that—but for his glory."

He said he was angry at God for about two months when he came out of the coma and realized what happened.

"But I'm a realist and knew how much work I had to do to get out of this screwed-up body," McPhillips said.

"There isn't a day that goes by that I don't think about Rob's (the man he killed in the head-on crash) death," he said. "It's like a knife sticking through my heart. Is there any way to put aside the knowledge that you caused another person to lose his life because of your own stupidity?"

But he tries to do what he can to teach others, who he hopes will learn from his mistakes. It is the core part of Scott McPhillips' third act.

Organizations wishing to contact McPhillips about a presentation can contact him and his mother at (712) 545-3003. His book and video are also available.

Web Site Heralds Man's Spiritual Recovery

by Tom McMahon, Staff Writer

Reprinted by permission from
The Daily Nonpareil, Tuesday, January 24, 2006

HONEY CREEK—A big red, blue and yellow S flashes across the computer screen with a whoosh. Superman fans recognize it immediately. Suddenly the man of steel's insignia cracks in two.

It's the opening to Scott McPhillips' Web site and he says an analogy for his life. The Honey Creek 36-year-old was an all-state athlete at Tri-Center High School, where he excelled in baseball, football and basketball. On Oct. 10, 1989, McPhillips was driving while high on drugs and alcohol and hit another car head on, killing its driver. He was in a nine-month coma following the accident and underwent extensive surgeries and rehabilitation.

In the midst of his physical recovery, McPhillips says he was also spiritually restored. He's written a book about his fall from earthly favor and spiritual birth. *"Superman Doesn't Live Here Anymore"*—and is working on a second, *"Superman Doesn't Live here Anymore II: Run to Jesus."*

"The first book glorified me a little," McPhillips confesses. "This one will have no pictures. I want to give Jesus all the glory."

He launched his Web-site, www.hey-scott.com, about three months ago as a way to try and reach others. The site includes his story, his message, a message board and information about the book.

"I want to break through to the world and tell people about God," McPhillips said. "I want to show them what he has done for me and show them the danger they put themselves in every time they use (drugs/alcohol)," he said. "I am sorry for my mistakes, for killing Rob, but I am trying to turn this around for God's glory."

McPhillips and his mother, Bev Krumwiede, have spoken to hundreds of groups since Scott's accident and recovery. They have several messages they send to listeners: Realize the dangers of drugs and alcohol, discover how faith in God can help heal body and soul, rediscover your values and what is important in life, appreciate good physical and mental health and retain a positive attitude while overcoming physical and emotional challenges.

McPhillips hopes to use the Web site to promote those same messages.

"I am on a mission. I want to make a difference in the world while I am in it," he said. "I am not living for this world now. I am heavenbound."

For more information, contact McPhillips at
(712) 545-4477, (712) 545-3003 or bkrumwiede@aol.com.

Give the gift of inspiration
To your friends and colleagues

ORDER HERE

YES, I want _____ copies of *Superman Doesn't Live Here II: Run to Jesus* at $10.00 paperback, plus $3.00 shipping per book, or three for $28.00 (Iowa residents please add $.60 tax per book). Allow 15 days for delivery.

My check or money order for $_____is enclosed.

Name _____

Phone _____

Organization _____

Address _____

City/State/Zip _____

Please make your check payable and return to

Mac on the Attack for Jesus
28535 Coldwater Avenue
Honey Creek, IA 51542

Call your order to: **(712) 545-4477 or (712) 545-3003**
Web site: hey-scott.com
E-mail: bkrumwiede@aol.com